Comedy of the Lost

Abdolhai Shammasi

TSL Drama

First published in Great Britain in 2022
By TSL Publications, Rickmansworth

ISBN: 978-1-914245-87-9

Cover design: Abbas Barghashi

Characters

OBOL – old man or woman, head of the Governate building

HOBOL – 35-year-old traveler, with a suitcase

WAITRESS – old, hobbles

DIGNIFIED MAN – dressed in rags

FAT WOMAN

HUNTER – thin bony man

GOVERNOR

Running Time

approx 60 mins

The events of drama take place in the waiting hall of the Governor-General building in a commercial town. All travelers come to the town only to shop and do business; so, they usually stay for a short while. The building has, in fact, been turned into a hostel with only one out of its 15 rooms allocated as the Governor's Office. The other rooms are often available for travelers. The title "Governor-General & Aram Hostel" appears on the doorway to the building. The atmosphere of the hostel [Governorate] is calm and quiet but a vague hubbub is heard from outside.

OBOL, the head of Governorate Office and the hostel as well, is an old man or woman who has fallen asleep behind the counter. There's a passage beside the counter which leads to the basement, a door is seen on the other side of the counter on top of which is a sign in illegible handwriting: "The Governorate will be off due to the warm weather." A passage leads to the kitchen.

Some couches and a table, each different in form and color, are in the middle of the waiting hall. None of the set props match each other in general.

The door is opened after some moments and HOBOL, a 35-year-old traveler, with a suitcase in his hand enters pell-mell. After a brief hesitation, he, horrified, looks outside through the half-closed door. He closes the door and heaves a sigh of relief while pushing the suitcase on his chest. He smiles with pleasure and says hello as he sees OBOL. He hears nothing in response. He goes closer and stands next to OBOL.

HOBOL: Hi! ... ha... ha... [Sneezes loudly.]

OBOL: [Awakes agitated and immediately pulls out a huge piece of stick from beneath the counter.] What? Who was it?

HOBOL: [Jumps back] Gee! ... It's me. Stop it...

OBOL: [Casts his eyes over HOBOL for a few seconds.] Don't be afraid... [Puts the stick on the counter, points his finger at HOBOL, indicating him to come closer.] Come on... Come closer... I won't hurt you.

HOBOL: Here... Is here a hostel?

OBOL: [Smiles.] As you wish.

HOBOL: [Looks around confusedly. Then, points at the signboard on the Governorate Office.] I mean... here...

OBOL: It's closed right now... But the hostel is open.

HOBOL: Excuse me... that...

OBOL: As if I was asleep... wasn't I?

HOBOL: Honestly... I've already arrived. I don't know.

OBOL: Yeah... I was asleep... That's right. Your voice awakened me.

HOBOL: I'm sorry... If I knew...

OBOL: Well... what would you do if you knew it? What?

HOBOL: I wouldn't awaken you.

OBOL: I thought so... [Picks up the stick.]

HOBOL:	[*Gets scared and steps back.*] Have I done something wrong?
OBOL:	You wanted to do so.
HOBOL:	Golly! ... What do you mean by that?
OBOL:	You're all wet... I made you stop.
HOBOL:	What do you think I wanted to do?
OBOL:	How shall I know? I was asleep.
HOBOL:	Yes... You were asleep... I just wanted to ask if there's a vacant room here. But...
OBOL:	Room!
HOBOL:	Uh-huh...
OBOL:	Ok... Come closer.
HOBOL:	[*Looks at the stick and hesitates to go closer.*] No, thanks... I'd better stay here.
OBOL:	[*Holds the stick under the counter.*] Don't be afraid... Come closer. But take your mind off all the evils...
HOBOL:	Surely not! ... Don't mention it...
OBOL:	[*Opens a big notebook on the counter.*] What's your name?
HOBOL:	Name! ... I don't know. Whatever you wish.
OBOL:	What? I asked about your name.
HOBOL:	I don't have any...
OBOL:	Don't you have any?
HOBOL:	No... It's been lost... I mean... How shall I say? I was robbed of my name...
OBOL:	What does that mean?
HOBOL:	I was robbed of it before I could know what happened.
OBOL:	[*Again takes out the stick from beneath the counter.*] Are you kidding me? You're in for it.
HOBOL:	[*Cowers.*] I... I eat humble pie.

OBOL:	[*Stands over* HOBOL *and raises the stick.*] May I beat you?
HOBOL:	No... I beg you.
OBOL:	[*Brings down the stick and goes toward the counter.*] Idiot...
HOBOL:	Yes... You're right.
OBOL:	[*Gets prepared to write down.*] Name?
HOBOL:	Name again? ... What shall I say? Which name do you like more?
OBOL:	[*Thinks.*] Which name?!
HOBOL:	Give it some thought...
OBOL:	I can't... Nothing comes to my mind.
HOBOL:	Give it a second try. Maybe you manage to... Look... [*He moves and mimics the mannequins in front of* OBOL.] Which name do you think suits me?
OBOL:	No idea... Which name would you really like for yourself?
HOBOL:	Depends on the name you'd like... Of course, it no longer matters to me...
OBOL:	Ok... My name is Obol. Would you like to be called Hobol?
HOBOL:	Hobol? Sounds great!
OBOL:	Yes... What else can be better than Hobol?
HOBOL:	[*Puts on airs and moves.*] Does it suit me?
OBOL:	Excellent! ... You don't have doubts about my good taste, do you? [*Writes down the name* HOBOL *in the notebook.*] Ho...bo...l.
HOBOL:	[*Cranes his neck to see how his name is written.*] It's a long time I've had no name.
OBOL:	[*Raises his head.*] No problem... You're called Hobol from now on.

HOBOL: [*Pleased.*] Yes... That's a weight off my mind now... Hobol... Hobol...

OBOL: Be appreciative of your name... I've chosen it in accordance with my own name.

HOBOL: Yes... quite clear... Hobol, Obol... Hobol, Obol...

OBOL: Nope... It's not fair... You're taking advantage of my name from the very beginning... You should first say Obol, then Hobol.

HOBOL: You're right. I'm sorry... Obol, Hobol... Obol, Hobol...

OBOL: That's it... It's not the way you think... I'm a very important person.

HOBOL: Quite clear... I know...

OBOL: [*Takes a thick file out of the drawer.*] Come and have a look... It's my serving file... Based on this Appointment Letter, I'm the Office Manager of the Governor.

HOBOL: Gee! ... Really?

OBOL: By the way ... look at this one... Maintaining the position, I'm the manager of "Aram Hostel" too.

HOBOL: Wow! ... Seems so many Appointment Letters!

OBOL: Right... All of them are Appointment Letters... Look at this one, for example... According to this Letter, I'm allowed to use this stick [*Takes the stick from beneath the counter at the same time.*] as I wish. [HOBOL *steps back again.*] Wait. Not finished yet...

HOBOL: Are the rest of the Letters related to the stick?

OBOL: No... this one, for instance... Come closer and listen. [*Reads the Letter.*] According to this Letter, you, [*Points at himself.*] that is, I... are noted that I order that Your Majesty, as my excellent consultant, has a big responsibility. I tell you every day to please go to the opposite pavement, that is on the other side of the street, and stand enthusiastically for several useful and exciting moments and look at the window glass of the Governorate building and smile joyfully and happily,

	then shake your head charmingly, and put your hands in the others' pockets, and if you light a cigarette and glance at the wooden timber…
HOBOL:	[*Begins yawning.*] What would happen then?
OBOL:	Wait… The other five pages have yet been left.
HOBOL:	Gosh!
OBOL:	Yes… when I stand before the building and take a look and do some funny things, people's attention will be attracted to the building and then more clients will be attracted… well… How can I help you?
HOBOL:	[*Agitates all of a sudden and says loudly in the way of seeking help.*] Oh my God! … They took away…
OBOL:	[*Shocked and raises the stick at once.*] What? Who?
HOBOL:	They took away all that I had… My ID card… my camera…
OBOL:	Get out of here… Seems you don't have money to rent a room.
HOBOL:	[*Turns quiet and stares at* OBOL *astonished.*] Money? I have money… as much as you wish…
OBOL:	Great…
HOBOL:	I'll find him at long last… I still remember his face.
OBOL:	Who was he who has left that suitcase?
HOBOL:	Suitcase… [*Pushes it on his chest.*] No… I bought it later.
OBOL:	[*Puts a big notebook in front of* HOBOL.] Sign here…
HOBOL:	ign! … Why?
OBOL:	You want a room, don't you?
HOBOL:	Right… yes… [*Without asking a questing or paying any attention, signs repeatedly where* OBOL *shows him.*] Here you are…
OBOL:	Your ID…
HOBOL:	ID? It's been stolen… as I said…
OBOL:	Well, how can I know who you are?

HOBOL:	[*Points at the suitcase.*] By this… That's inside it.
OBOL:	Inside it?
HOBOL:	Yeah… I know who am I by this.
OBOL:	So, give it to me.
HOBOL:	No… I don't.
OBOL:	Don't you? Ok. I don't provide you with a room here either.
HOBOL:	My number will be up if I lose it.
OBOL:	Up to you… That's a must.
HOBOL:	Must! … You're kidding.
OBOL:	Nothing is done here haphazardly… I have an official letter for it… I can't disobey it.
HOBOL:	[*Brings his head forward.*] Do something… [*Looks around.*] You know what I mean, don't you? [*Takes something out of his pocket and holds it out secretly to OBOL.*] Nobody can know in this hustle and bustle.
OBOL:	[*With a serious tone.*] Stop whispering in my ear… I don't want to lose my prestige at any cost…
HOBOL:	[*Cowers.*] Please… I didn't want to hurt you.
OBOL:	Be honest… What do you have in that suitcase?
HOBOL:	Sign… With the help of it, I no longer get lost among the hustle and bustle of the town.
OBOL:	You've got lost anyway… It's chaotic here… One comes in, another one goes out… One comes in, another one goes out… All come here just to do business and make money.
HOBOL:	[*Talks to himself.*] They robbed… They stole what I had in the hustle and bustle…
OBOL:	It's a dog-eat-dog world out there! … They'll pick your pocket in a jiffy… [*Points at the suitcase.*] Well… show me who you are.
HOBOL:	[*Hesitates for a second.*] Come closer… [*Looks around. Then brings his head closer and says something quietly*

in OBOL's *ear.* OBOL's *jaw drops with his eyes wide open.*] Got it?

OBOL: Really? Is it a special kind too?

HOBOL: Aha... [*Opens his arms wide to show a great size.*] This much.

OBOL: Seems too big! ... I think the one belonging to the Governor is as big as this.

HOBOL: Governor!

OBOL: Yeah... I saw it in his office.

HOBOL: What a surprise!

OBOL: Why do you get surprised? He's put it in a corner of his office. I saw it myself... You can't forget or help liking it once you see him...

HOBOL: Well, when can I meet him?

OBOL: Have you made an appointment?

HOBOL: No... Who can help me do it?

OBOL: Me... The Governor accepts nobody without an appointment.

HOBOL: Ok... Could you please schedule an appointment for me?

OBOL: [*Browses through the calendar on the counter.*] In nine months' time...

HOBOL: Nine month?! Am I going to be born?

OBOL: It's not possible for you to meet him sooner.

HOBOL: Is it something usual? ... Can't I meet him sooner?

OBOL: No... The Governorate office will be closed till then... But don't worry. I've provided you with the earliest.

HOBOL: Where is here then? Till then, they would rob even myself.

OBOL: Shh! ... Stop raising your voice at me! ... This is the Governorate office and an honorable hostel as well.

HOBOL:	Do you mean here is honorable? Anyway… Anyway… They steal anything you have.
OBOL:	Is that so… [*Cautiously goes toward the telephone.*] Sounds great!
HOBOL:	[*Screams loudly all of a sudden.*] Aah!
OBOL:	[*Startles, takes up the stick hastily, and begins shouting.*] Eh… Eh!
HOBOL:	I forgot it at long last.
OBOL:	[*Attacks* HOBOL *with the stick.* HOBOL *tries to escape but falls down.* OBOL *stands over* HOBOL *and raises the stick.*] I'll hit you over the head…
HOBOL:	No… please…
OBOL:	[*Pauses just for a moment. Then brings down the stick.*] You scared me to death…
HOBOL:	Why do you raise the stick under any circumstances?
OBOL:	[*Goes behind the counter and puts the stick beneath the counter. Tries to pretend he's calm.*] Be at ease.
HOBOL:	I'm at ease… but it seems that you…
OBOL:	No… nothing important… I'm just a bit nervous…
HOBOL:	You're right… Such a crowded town takes everything away from you, let alone calmness… By the way, you wanted to call someone, didn't you?
OBOL:	It doesn't matter… I forgot it.
HOBOL:	You're right… Seems good that you still remember your own name in such a situation.
OBOL:	You're Hobol… Try not to forget it.
HOBOL:	You're Obol. Am I right?
OBOL:	Right…
HOBOL:	What a pity I was robbed of all my stuff.
OBOL:	That's because you're a good-for-nothing.

HOBOL: No... no... I'm not good-for-nothing. They're too handy... They behaved in a way so that I was deceived... They can deceive anybody.

The old WAITRESS, *hobbling lamely and slowly, enters the stage from the end of the passage. She holds a tray in her hand on which there's some rice. She sits down and begins removing pebbles from rice without saying anything.*

OBOL: Isn't there anywhere else?

WAITRESS: What?

OBOL: I am asking if there isn't anywhere else? Why don't you do it in the kitchen?

WAITRESS: It's dark there. I can't see well.

OBOL: None of my business... You see there's a client here, don't you? I wouldn't like anybody bothering him...

HOBOL: No problem. She doesn't bother me at all...

OBOL: Shut up!... Who asked your opinion? If I am the boss here, I know better what is good or bad.

HOBOL: I'm sorry. I just...

OBOL: Rules... Look! ... [*Browses through the files.*] According to this official letter, I'm not allowed to let anybody remove pebbles from rice here.

HOBOL: Excuse me... I didn't know you're acting according to the rules... You see, I'm just a newcomer.

OBOL: Well, don't meddle... I should make myself understood.

HOBOL: Do you want to beat her?

OBOL: No... I'm going to punish her according to the rules.

WAITRESS: [*Scared.*] No... No blood has left in my veins.

OBOL: [*Takes a large jar out of the wardrobe.*] My darlings...

WAITRESS: No... please... My eyes have already started to blur.

HOBOL: What are they?

WAITRESS: Leeches...

OBOL: [*Puts the jar on the counter and looks at the leeches joyfully.*] What's wrong with you? Are you starving again? You've already eaten up.

WAITRESS: A pile of pebbles is seen among rice grains... I can't recognize them in the kitchen... It's too dark.

OBOL: According to this official Letter, I should punish you.

WAITRESS: Please... All the time, I'm feeling dizzy... and shaking in the knees.

OBOL: You can pay for it instead... Ok?

WAITRESS: Yes... I'll work 10 days without being paid...

OBOL: [*Opens a notebook and writes.*] Up to now, it's about 27 years and 2 months and 13 days and 11 hours...

HOBOL: 27 years and...

OBOL: Right... I've rounded it down by the way.

WAITRESS: You're going to swindle me... I've been keeping count of it. I'm only 25 years and 4 months and 10 days in debt up to now, not 27...

OBOL: Well, what about the penalty charge? Can you afford to pay it all?

HOBOL: [*Brings his head closer and says to* OBOL.] Do you think she can afford to pay off her debt?

OBOL: She has to...

HOBOL: Do you think that she would stay alive till then?

OBOL: Trust... optimism... So, there are some people who want to take advantage of me.

WAITRESS: There is a pile of pebbles...

OBOL: Do your job.

WAITRESS: It shouldn't be full of pebbles.

HOBOL: Mice droppings! ... What if there are some mice droppings among the rice grains?

WAITRESS: Then, it would be better to throw away all the rice.

OBOL: [*To the* WAITRESS] Go back and sit there... [*To* HOBOL.] Shh! ... Go and stand next to the wall.

WAITRESS: [*Picks up the tray and hobbles lamely toward the passage. Then, stops and turns back.*] Just one mouse dropping turns all the rice useless.

The WAITRESS *leaves the stage.* HOBOL *is standing beside the wall.* OBOL *takes the jar of leeches and puts it back in the wardrobe.*

OBOL: [*Points at* HOBOL.] Come closer now... To let you stay here, I must know who you are.

HOBOL: [*Lifts the suitcase.*] You mean with the help of this then...

OBOL: It's too big.

HOBOL: Well, ok...

OBOL: Well, where shall I put it?

HOBOL: Don't worry about it. Leave it to me... By the way, come closer... [*Says something in* OBOL's *ear.*]

OBOL: Rope!

HOBOL: Yeah... Two metres please.

OBOL: Have you thought it over?

HOBOL: There's no way out... It's the best way but it should be a strong rope... You see, it'll be all over with me if the rope is broken.

OBOL: Set your mind at ease. We provide our clients with the best services here.

HOBOL: Thanks indeed... You're well aware of the pain I'm suffering. I can't tolerate it anymore... As if I am nobody. I can get rid of this situation if I access a strong rope.

OBOL: I understand you well.

HOBOL: I have neither a name... nor a job... I just... have money...

OBOL: I'll fix it up for you... You have a name now. Haven't forgotten, have you? Hobol...

HOBOL:	Yes. But I need a piece of rope right now... I'll bother you later for a job and stuff like that... But that rope...
OBOL:	Sounds great that you keep your word... Wait a moment. [*Takes a piece of black rope from the wardrobe and holds it out to* HOBOL.] Come on... Here's the rope...
HOBOL:	Thanks... [*Gets the rope and tries it.*] Doesn't it break?
OBOL:	Be sure... It's just like a towrope.
HOBOL:	Excellent!
OBOL:	Do you know how many people have been saved by this rope?
HOBOL:	Good for them...
OBOL:	Yeah... [*Takes the rope and moves one of the ends in front of* HOBOL; *the end with a noose for hanging.*] I mean this noose... Whoever wants to use it, rents one of the rooms at the end of the hallway.
HOBOL:	[*Draws back slightly.*] But... But I...
OBOL:	[*Pulls the rope.*] It's too strong... [*Holds out it to* HOBOL.] Come on... Give it a try.
HOBOL:	No... No. I believe you.
OBOL:	It was just last week that one of the travelers failed to knot the rope perfectly... Do you know what happened then?
HOBOL:	[*Speechless with fear.*] No... No...
OBOL:	He fell on his back as he began hanging himself... Poor man... Now, he's feeling too bad. It's left him paralyzed from the waist down. At first, everybody put the blame on me. After coming in, he confessed that he'd failed to knot the rope tightly... To be honest, I really felt deep pity for him since he stayed alive... He fell from the frying pan into the fire.
HOBOL:	How good that he didn't die...

OBOL: He didn't?! What did you think then? Now that poor guy has to keep on living and die more than once.

The door opens and a DIGNIFIED MAN *dressed in torn rags enters. He stops for a while and then goes forward.*

DIG. MAN: Hello…

OBOL: Hello, sir… You're welcome here.

DIG. MAN: Right… I'm welcome here. Here is Aram Hostel… am I right?

OBOL: Yes, sir… Here it is…

DIG. MAN: How nice! … [*Looks around.*] So, can you help me?

OBOL: Yes, for sure… How can I help you?

DIG. MAN: I want a room to stay… for a night.

OBOL: At the end of the hallway?

DIG. MAN: Right… [*Stares at the rope.*] What an amazing rope! … Do you have just this one?

OBOL: No, sir… We have as many as you wish.

HOBOL: [*Pushes the rope toward the man.*] Here you are. I didn't want it.

OBOL: Take it…

DIG. MAN: [*To* HOBOL.] My friend, you too…

OBOL: He's going to deal with something else.

DIG. MAN: Oh, yes… Do you know? I always wondered why it turns out to be so… or what's really the reason behind it… [*To* HOBOL.] What do you think about it?

HOBOL: [*Having been confused.*] Think?

DIG. MAN: Well, you haven't yet figured it out either… I'm so sorry… You don't know… You don't know…

When the black birds fly
Over the blueness of the sea
A heart is broken at night
There's not a dried bread in the collapsed walls' cracks.
And a mother, lying in the cold bed

Her child, alone and hungry
At the mother's bed
Has been left, longing for
His father to come back
And the father came back
With his hands full,
With his hands full of blisters and pain.

OBOL: That's the advantage of this town... I mean anybody can live his own life as he wishes and refrains from meddling in others' affairs.

DIG. MAN: Yes! ... Even that poor child? Is it really possible that the child is born once more?

OBOL: I have no idea.

DIG. MAN: What about the Governor...? Doesn't he know either?

OBOL: Do you mean Mr Governor? Yes, he certainly knows... As you said, a governor should essentially know what's going on in the town... By the way, since the Governorate office is always responding to clients' questions and providing newly arrived travelers with suitable rooms in order for them not to need to provide the relation of the brief tangible supplies for buying the needed stuff and selling properties...

DIG. MAN: Wait... Wait... I didn't understand the last sentence you said.

HOBOL: Me neither...

DIG. MAN: ... To provide the relation of the brief tangible supplies ... [*Thinks for a while and murmurs.*] No... I don't understand.

OBOL: The rope... Did you forget it?

DIG. MAN: Oh, I'm so sorry... I've already reached a very attractive conclusion... I try to say it in simple words... It's a kind of feeling of course.

HOBOL: How nice!

DIG. MAN: Nice?! I don't know... I feel that I'm so strong... That's why I should feel happy... I don't know if you understand what I mean... Not everybody could have such a feeling... Now I can make up my mind about the greatest event in my whole life... Sounds great, doesn't it?

OBOL: [*Tries a rope.*] Seems excellent...

HOBOL: Can I?

DIG. MAN: You! ... It's up to you.

HOBOL: By the way... didn't anybody pick your pocket on your way here?

DIG. MAN: No, sir... I'm still thinking about the last sentence you said... to provide the relation of...

HOBOL: But I was robbed of all my stuff.

DIG. MAN: They weren't poor, were they?

HOBOL: No, sir... They were thieves.

DIG. MAN: Yes, it should be this way... [*To* OBOL.] To provide the relation of the brief tangible supplies...

OBOL: Yes... That's it.

DIG. MAN: I feel that this sentence strengthens me much more... Yes... I feel I'm stronger than before... [*To* OBOL.] Dear friend, you made me feel much more strength by saying this sentence... I feel that I can better make serious decisions now.

OBOL: Never mind... I do just my duties. [*Still playing with the rope.*]

DIG. MAN: Great! ... Has the Governor heard this sentence too?

OBOL: I don't know... maybe.

DIG. MAN: Well, please ask him about it...

OBOL: Yes... [*Picks up the phone and begins dialing a number.*] You're right. He should know... No, he doesn't answer the phone.

HOBOL: He won't answer. Here is written that it's closed.

OBOL:	I can see it myself.
DIG. MAN:	How interesting! … Well, where did you dial then?
OBOL:	The zoo…
DIG. MAN:	Sounds interesting!
HOBOL:	Quite clear… He's busy with the animals. That's why they robbed me of all my stuff.
OBOL:	Keep quiet… Why don't you leave here?
HOBOL:	I don't have a room yet.
OBOL:	You should hold an ID card if you want to stay in a room here.
DIG. MAN:	Oh… yes. The same rule surely applies to me too.
OBOL:	Yes, with all due respect…
DIG. MAN:	[*Takes a pile of ID cards out of his pocket and puts them on the counter.*] Here you are… I've got nothing but these… Take them.
OBOL:	[*Picks up the cards.*] Great!
DIG. MAN:	You can hold all of them… I don't need them anymore.
HOBOL:	Well, what about me?
DIG. MAN:	You?
OBOL:	[*Ties one end of the rope to a big key.*] Here you are, sir… Room 11, at the end of the hallway.
DIG. MAN:	Thank you… At the end of the hallway… Would you please tell me now the meaning of the last sentence you said?
OBOL:	Go to the hallway, I'll say it to you.
DIG. MAN:	[*To* HOBOL.] Well, dear friend…
HOBOL:	[*Acts hastily.*] You…
DIG. MAN:	I'm tired… I'm zonked out.
OBOL:	The room is ready, sir…
DIG. MAN:	Thank you… [*Murmurs to himself while walking away.*] To provide the relation of the brief tangible supplies…

The DIGNIFIED MAN *walks up the stairs. Then stops at the beginning of the hallway, looks at the audience, and bursts into loud laughter. He stops laughing and leaves the stage in a serious mood. HOBOL, scared, lifts his suitcase and starts walking toward the hostel's entrance. Near the door, he stops as he hears OBOL's voice.*

OBOL: Where are you going?

HOBOL: I changed my mind... I don't want a room.

OBOL: There's no other hostel in the town.

HOBOL: He went to...

OBOL: Don't bother yourself...

HOBOL: Ok... I stay in this hall.

OBOL: Until when?

HOBOL: I'll stay till... I'll stay... I...

OBOL: Here is the waiting hall. You'll have to choose one of these two ways... Outside or at the end of the hallway...

HOBOL: Outside?! Everything is in a mess out there.

OBOL: You can stay here... providing that you open up that suitcase right now.

HOBOL: The suitcase?

OBOL: Right... Or I'll take the name Hobol back from you and throw you out of here.

HOBOL: No... I want to open the suitcase when I've found somewhere to stay.

OBOL: You've already found it... Get it out...

HOBOL *puts the suitcase on the counter and opens it. The inside of the suitcase is out of sight of the audience. OBOL screams out of surprise as the suitcase is opened.*

OBOL: What...a surprise!

HOBOL: How beautiful it is, isn't it?

OBOL: So much! ... May I touch it?

HOBOL: Ok, but be careful!

OBOL: [*Inserts his hand cautiously inside the suitcase and takes out a big pumpkin.*] Gee... how big it is! ...

HOBOL: By having this, it's no longer possible that I get lost.

OBOL: [*Lifts the pumpkin and looks at it from beneath.*] Can't be any better!

HOBOL: I searched all around to find it...

OBOL: [*Stretches his hand forward and shakes* HOBOL*'s hand.*] I really congratulate you.

HOBOL: Thanks so much...

OBOL: I didn't think at all that the case was that much serious and important.

HOBOL: Yes... and vital as well.

OBOL: How good it would be if all of us had such a great and reliable sign.

HOBOL: You mean all the same in shape?

OBOL: Not exactly... One, for example, an eggplant... One, a melon, a beet... Everyone must own something special anyway...

HOBOL: How good it would be... But no. So many problems would happen this way.

OBOL: Problem?

HOBOL: What if someone's portion is a little fruit-like cherry?

OBOL: Nobody is to blame. Everybody deserves to have something for himself.

HOBOL: Then I deserve to have the biggest one this way.

OBOL: [*Takes out the pumpkin again, raises it and moves around the stage.*] How great!

The sound of a door opening is heard. HOBOL *gets the pumpkin back quickly, puts it in the suitcase, and closes it. The voice of a woman at the door is heard.*

FAT WOMAN: [*Voice only is heard.*] Oh! ... Why are you moving that much? Bend a little more and let me get off... Aha... Stay away and let me pass... How nice you are, dear...

The door opens. First, a FAT WOMAN enters with a fan in her hand. After her, the HUNTER who is her husband enters. The HUNTER is a thin bony man who carries a howdah on his shoulders with many suitcases hanging around it. The face and head of the HUNTER are hidden behind the suitcases.

FAT WOMAN: [To the HUNTER.] My darling... come on... come and stand here. [Goes forward and stares at HOBOL for a relatively long time.]

HOBOL: [Pestered under the FAT WOMAN's gaze, beckons to OBOL by moving his head and hands.] The owner of here...

FAT WOMAN: Who asked you?

HOBOL: Sorry...

FAT WOMAN: No need at all... Who are you?

HOBOL: I'm Hobol...

FAT WOMAN: None of my business what your name is... Go away...

HOBOL: Gee!

OBOL: [To the FAT WOMAN.] Don't upset yourself over it... He's crazy.

HOBOL steps back and approaches the HUNTER. Walks around the HUNTER once and looks at him carefully.

FAT WOMAN: How rude you are!

OBOL: Never mind... please.

FAT WOMAN: How strange... Here is a hostel, isn't it?

OBOL: Right, ma'am... You're looking for somewhere quiet and cozy, aren't you?

FAT WOMAN: Right... Somewhere quiet and cozy...

OBOL: Great... For you yourself?

FAT WOMAN: Gee! ... Don't you see? [To the HUNTER with some feminine gestures.] For my husband...

OBOL: Husband! ... Which?

FAT WOMAN: He's too tired, poor guy... [*Approaches the* HUNTER.] Are you tired, my darling?

HUNTER: I'm tired... When will we reach then?

FAT WOMAN: Be patient, my dear... I tolerate all these difficulties just for the sake of you. [*Goes toward* OBOL.] Do you know? He's my whole life... I love him to the moon and back.

OBOL: Good for him... What a devoted wife he has...

FAT WOMAN: What a nice man... Today is the 24th anniversary of our marriage.

HOBOL: 24 years!

FAT WOMAN: Yes... but the private life of the others has got nothing to do with you.

HOBOL: You're right... I'm sorry... [*Murmurs.*] 24 years... Poor guy! ... [*Approaches the* HUNTER. *Walks around him once and looks at him.*] Hey... where are you?

HUNTER: I'm here... Where are you?

HOBOL: Gee... don't you see me?

HUNTER: You don't see me either.

HOBOL: I see just a howdah and a lot of suitcases.

HUNTER: You're right... I'm behind the suitcases and under the howdah... Are you under the howdah and behind the suitcases like me?

HOBOL: No... I have only one suitcase.

HUNTER: Sounds great! ... I have no suitcases.

HOBOL: Well, what are all these?

HUNTER: I've got no suitcase.

HOBOL: Good for you... That's good... It's very nice that you carry just a light load.

HUNTER: I feel tired... I'm getting crushed.

HOBOL: Why don't you get out?

HUNTER: I can't...

HOBOL: Would you like me to help you?

HUNTER: Help! ... What do you mean by that?

OBOL: [*Shows the* HUNTER *out.*] How strange!

FAT WOMAN: What's wrong with it?

OBOL: You shouldn't let your husband mingle with strangers.

HOBOL: [*Checks the suitcases.*] You can see me if you move your head from behind the suitcases.

HUNTER: How do you look?

FAT WOMAN: Hey, sir... Why are you bothering my husband?

HOBOL: [*Goes toward the* FAT WOMAN.] Excuse me, ma'am... May I ask a question?

FAT WOMAN: Oh! ... You're so corny...

HOBOL: Are you sure he's been a loyal husband during these 24 years?

FAT WOMAN: Oh! ... Did he tell you anything?

HOBOL: No, I couldn't find his head to talk with him.

FAT WOMAN: My husband has never gone anywhere without me... I mean, he can't live without me even for a moment.

HUNTER: Where is here? [*Tries to bend.*]

FAT WOMAN: No... No, my dear. You shouldn't move a lot or you get tired.

HUNTER: Well, when will we reach?

FAT WOMAN: Hold on just a little while longer... please, my dear.

HUNTER: You always say that.

FAT WOMAN: [*Turns to* OBOL.] You don't know how tender-hearted he is... He's full of emotion and passion. Even a simple word makes him gloomy. Of course, he's right. All artists are the same.

HOBOL: Artist! ... [*Regretfully.*] What a pity I don't have a camera with me.

HUNTER: I used to be a hunter before being crushed under such a load.

FAT WOMAN: But now, he's an artist... He tells both stories and poems...

OBOL: Yes... artists are too sensitive.

FAT WOMAN: Do you know them then?

OBOL: Yes, ma'am... Nobody can know people better than a hostel manager.

FAT WOMAN: Well, you judge how difficult and intolerable it is to live with them.

OBOL: Yes... it's really agonizing.

FAT WOMAN: He's suffering from so many diseases just because of being highly sensitive... I mean high blood pressure, gastritis, peptic and duodenal ulcer, high blood urea, and...

OBOL: Right... all artists are suffering from kinds of diseases.

FAT WOMAN: They can never calm down.

HOBOL: Is he still busy hunting?

FAT WOMAN: Hunting!

HUNTER: I can't go hunting anymore... I've forgotten everything since I was crushed under such a load.

FAT WOMAN: It's me who shoulders the burden of all difficulties.

OBOL: Right... you shouldn't bother yourself anymore.

FAT WOMAN: Only my love toward him has made me tolerate that many difficulties.

OBOL: Now it's time for him to take a rest.

HOBOL: [*Lifts his suitcase laying in front of the* FAT WOMAN.] Excuse me.

FAT WOMAN: Oh! ... How impolite you are... Do you think I'm that kind of a person?!

HOBOL: I didn't really mean to bother you... I'd better take my leave and go to sleep.

OBOL: Wait... I have to fix things for this lady first.

FAT WOMAN: O, sir! ... No trace of politeness and manliness is seen anymore.

HOBOL: No problem... I'll keep waiting. After you, ma'am.

HUNTER: Well, what's happened? Haven't we reached there yet?

FAT WOMAN: Be patient, dear... I'm trying to provide you with a life of comfort and ease... [*Turns to* OBOL.] Do you see? He always keeps nagging.

OBOL: Be patient, ma'am... You've been patient for 24 years, keep waiting just for a while more.

FAT WOMAN: Take a look yourself... He keeps on moving apropos of nothing... He can't hold still for a moment.

OBOL: God save me from folks.

FAT WOMAN: But I'm a devoted wife. To take it easy, we go on honeymoon every year so that he can always feel young.

HOBOL: Honeymoon?! Sounds great!

FAT WOMAN: Oh! ... You've been on honeymoon so far, haven't you?

HOBOL: [*Holds his suitcase tightly and kisses it.*] Long live pumpkin...

FAT WOMAN: What a nonsense! ... [*Turns to the* HUNTER *but addresses* OBOL.] I can't tolerate that he has a hard time... I'm fed up with him. To be honest, sometimes I'd like to leave him but I can't find it in my heart to do so.

HOBOL: [*To the* HUNTER.] Hey... is it too heavy?

HUNTER: I've got used to it.

HOBOL: Would you like to get out?

FAT WOMAN: [*Goes forward hurriedly.*] What are you doing? Why do you make him tired by your nonsense words?

HOBOL: We were just talking.

FAT WOMAN: Talking! ... What do you have in common to talk about? He's resting.

HOBOL: Just a moment, I'll...

FAT WOMAN: [*To the* HUNTER.] My darling... Did his words bother you?

HUNTER: I'm tired...

FAT WOMAN: [*To* OBOL.] Look... how he's lost his voice... Please hurry up. He should rest right now... A nice and comfortable room... a room where he can feel calm.

OBOL: A nice and comfortable room, at the end of hallway.

FAT WOMAN: [*Coquettishly.*] At the end of hallway...

HUNTER: No... a room with a window, please.

OBOL: You can see no landscape through the window... The end of hallway is ok.

FAT WOMAN: He's right, my dear... The end of hallway is ok.

HOBOL: [*Quietly to the* HUNTER.] Don't buy into it... The room with a window...

FAT WOMAN: What did you say?

HOBOL: Nothing... I just asked if he's ok.

FAT WOMAN: He's ok... Take care of yourself, you skinny.

HUNTER: I'm tired...

FAT WOMAN: Don't worry, darling... It'll be finished.

OBOL: [*Takes a rope out of the wardrobe.*] The room is ready...

FAT WOMAN: [*To* HUNTER.] Don't bother yourself please, darling... [*Turns to* OBOL.] Are the rooms at the end of hallway quiet and comfortable?

OBOL: Yes, ma'am... Quiet and comfortable.

FAT WOMAN: You'll be relaxed within a few hours... [*Turns to* OBOL.] Do you know? I've never let my husband have a bad time... I can't find it in my heart to let his room not be comfortable.

OBOL: You can come and check the rooms at the end of hallway if you worry about it.

FAT WOMAN: Ok... I know well my husband's temperament. I'd like
to do his room decoration myself... [*To* HOBOL.] Gee! ...
Why are you staring at me like this?

HOBOL: Uh!

FAT WOMAN: Seems you have nothing else to do.

HOBOL: I do... I do... [*Sits at a corner and addresses* OBOL.] I'll
stay here.

OBOL: I'll provide you with a place as soon as I come back.

FAT WOMAN: My darling... don't mingle with the strangers... I'm
going to spruce up your room.

The FAT WOMAN *walks up the stairs along with* OBOL *and they leave
the stage. The* HUNTER *moves slightly after a few moments.* HOBOL
raises his head and stares at him.

HUNTER: Did they leave?

HOBOL: Yeah... Come out...

HUNTER: Good... [*Comes out cautiously. Tries to get refreshed by
moving his head, neck, and hands.*] Ouch! ... I've been
crushed.

HOBOL: Seems they're too heavy, doesn't it?

HUNTER: You can figure out what the word heavy really means if
you shoulder and have to carry them around once for
all...

HOBOL: Well, what are there in these suitcases?

HUNTER: I don't know...

HOBOL: Are you obliged? Leave her alone.

HUNTER: Do you mean I leave her alone?! No, I can't.

HOBOL: It doesn't matter at all. Don't buy into it.

HUNTER: It's a long time I've tolerated the heavy burden of this
howdah and its owner.

HOBOL: Are all the suitcases hers?

HUNTER: Yeah...

HOBOL: What's in them?

HUNTER: They've been closed all the time... I wanted to open them a couple of times but I failed.

HOBOL: What do you think if we open them now?

HUNTER: Ok... But how?

HOBOL: Very easy... with the key.

HUNTER: I don't have the key... Besides, I don't know why I fear to open them.

HOBOL: No need to fear... I'll open them for you. [*Wants to lift one of the suitcases but despite trying, he can't move it at all. He tries another one but he fails again.*] Wow! ... As if they're glued to the ground! ... They are really heavy... How can you carry all these loads? It's as if all loads in the world have been gathered in these suitcases.

HUNTER: These aren't that heavy yet... My chest is about to burst from the pressure when she herself sat on the howdah... Come and have a look... [*Shows his shoulders.*]

HOBOL: Wow! ... [*Turns back.*]

HUNTER: I'm almost prostrate with these injuries.

HOBOL: You are a champion...

HUNTER: Champion! ... Champion? Once, there was a champion whose power was unique in the world. He had traveled a lot, lifted the greatest rocks in the world, and wrestled all the famous champions to the ground... He was the world's greatest champion. Once he decided to pass through a loop when he noticed that there was no other rock to lift and no champion to wrestle to the ground... He went into the loop but he could no longer get out of it... I wrote this story long time ago.

HOBOL: What a strange tale!

HUNTER: It's a bitter story... like many other tales.

HOBOL: You know so many tales like this, don't you?

HUNTER: Right... I know the story of a hunter who has got stuck in a trap himself.

HOBOL: How does the story end?

HUNTER: Who knows? I remember so many stories as I take the suitcases off my shoulders... I'd better fetch something to open the suitcases. [*After a few steps, he twists his ankle and falls down.*] Ouch!

HOBOL: [*Goes toward the* HUNTER.] Why are you walking like this then?

HUNTER: [*Gets up assisted by* HOBOL.] I knew... I knew that I couldn't walk even a step further without carrying those loads.

HOBOL: [*Helps the* HUNTER *sit on the couch.*] Come on... Come here and sit.

HUNTER: Did you see? I can't walk anymore... My feet have got used to all those loads. To walk, I should feel the pressure of that howdah on my shoulders.

HOBOL: Well, there's no need to walk now...

HUNTER: Whenever the howdah is on my shoulders, the suitcases obstruct my view... Sometimes I forget what people look like...

HOBOL: There must be some valuable things inside the suitcases.

HUNTER: God save me from the locked suitcases... the ones nobody knows what is inside them.

HOBOL: Whoever I saw all around the town was carrying a suitcase on his shoulders.

HUNTER: There was all hubbub around...

Approaching footsteps are heard. The HUNTER *gets up hastily, goes under the howdah, and puts it on his shoulders. After a few moments, the* WAITRESS *enters with the tray of rice in her hands.*

WAITRESS: A pile of pebbles is seen among rice grains.

HOBOL: Haven't you finished with it yet?

WAITRESS: I've lost my vision. I can no longer see as clear as before. [*Gets busy removing pebbles from rice.*] Nobody cares about it either.

HOBOL: [*To the* HUNTER.] Come out... The waitress is coming.

HUNTER: No... I'd better be careful.

HOBOL: Don't you get bored under that load?

HUNTER: No... I'm thinking instead.

HOBOL: What are you thinking about then?

HUNTER: Nothing right now... but I'm going to think about why that champion has still failed to pass through the loop.

WAITRESS: A pile of pebbles is seen among the rice grains... Anybody would think that rice is equally pebble this way.

HOBOL: But rice is rice... pebble is pebble too.

WAITRESS: But now they've mixed so much that you can't separate them easily.

HOBOL: Right... Everything has become snarled all around.

WAITRESS: I should be careful, or I must throw the whole lot away.

HOBOL: Right... but do you see that poor guy? Now he can't see anything and has to think instead.

WAITRESS: Poor guy!

HOBOL: Yeah... Poor guy can't walk, see, and think either. He has to just walk or think or see...

WAITRESS: Gee! ... What a troubled man!

HOBOL: Now he's found beneath there a cozy place to think.

WAITRESS: [*Holds out the tray to* HOBOL.] Look if there's still left any pebbles.

HOBOL: [*Gets the tray and mixes the rice ignorantly.*] No... I don't think so. They all resemble each other.

WAITRESS: Well, you've lost your vision too... A pile of pebbles has been mixed with the rice.

HOBOL: [*Gives the tray back to the* WAITRESS.] Well, why do you give it to me if you have clear eyesight yourself?

WAITRESS: Because I've lost my vision but I know that a pile of pebbles is among the rice grains... You neither can see well nor know the difference between rice and pebble.

HOBOL: I saw no pebbles.

WAITRESS: That's why we face all these adversities.

HUNTER: Hey! ... Isn't anybody around here?

HOBOL: Just that guy... He says that he used to be a hunter before but he's telling poems now. [*Goes toward the* HUNTER.] Did you hear our words?

HUNTER: Which words?

HOBOL: About the pebbles among the rice grains...

HUNTER: I was busy thinking.

HOBOL: Great! ... What were you thinking about?

HUNTER: Do you have a suitcase too?

HOBOL: Yeah... it's good you remind me.

HUNTER: Is it heavy?

HOBOL: So-so... You can move it anyway.

HUNTER: [*Takes out his head cautiously.*] May I come out?

HOBOL: Yeah... She's somehow an insider.

HUNTER: [*Comes out and looks carefully at* HOBOL's *suitcase.*] What a nice suitcase! ... What is there inside it?

HOBOL: [*Holds out his finger to his nose as if to say be quiet.*] Shh! ... A pumpkin... a pumpkin... It's my sign.

HUNTER: [*Begins laughing.*] Pumpkin?!

HOBOL: Be quiet... you, poor guy. You wouldn't get into hot water if you, like me, bought a pumpkin and held it against yourself from the very beginning.

HUNTER: Well, a pumpkin...

HOBOL: What else? It's the best sign in such a lawless town.

HUNTER: Ridiculous!

HOBOL: You are ridiculous because you don't know where you are and what to do. You can understand what's going on if you get out of there and look around.

HUNTER: [*Pauses for a while.*] Maybe... the most ridiculous thing in such total chaos seems to be the wisest choice.

WAITRESS: No... impossible. It isn't proved so easily.

HOBOL: [*Takes the pumpkin out of the suitcase.*] Look... By having this, I'm not scared of getting lost anymore.

HUNTER: Well, what can you do with it?

HOBOL: I fasten it to my leg.

HUNTER: Well... So, why don't you fasten it? You said that you'd get lost otherwise, didn't you?

HOBOL: I did... As if it's the right time to do so... [*Fastens the pumpkin to his leg with a rope.*] How does it look? Does it suit me?

HUNTER: Yeah... the rope might be wrapped around your leg and make you trip and fall.

HOBOL: You're right... Why didn't that come to my own mind?

HUNTER: Quite clear... You can't step forward if you fasten your leg to something with a rope.

HOBOL: Nothing else came to my mind... I'm scared of getting lost.

HUNTER: Me too... We should think about another solution.

HOBOL: [*Picks up the pumpkin from the ground.*] Say, how would it be if I hold the pumpkin tightly in my arms?

HUNTER: The rope is still fastened to your leg anyway... This way, your hands would be tied up too.

HOBOL: This pumpkin was my last hope... Then, who would recognize who I am if I don't tie it to myself? I would get lost... I've been robbed of all my stuff... I have nothing to prove who I am...

HUNTER: Don't bother yourself... There must be another way out
            of it.

HOBOL: No way out... Good for you that there's someone who
            takes care of you... but what about me?

The GOVERNOR *enters. The* HUNTER *goes hastily under the howdah
and lifts it as the* GOVERNOR *steps in.* HOBOL *holds the pumpkin
tightly in his arms and tries to pretend he's calm. The* WAITRESS
leaves before the GOVERNOR *sees her. After closing the door, the*
GOVERNOR *looks at the people standing there one by one and smiles
as he sees* HOBOL. HOBOL *startles as he sees the* GOVERNOR. *Then
he puts the pumpkin on the ground and, as a cat goes toward its prey,
approaches the* GOVERNOR. *The* GOVERNOR *steps back.*

GOVERNOR: Oh! ... What are you going?

HOBOL: [*Attacks the* GOVERNOR *all of a sudden and catches
            him.*] Aha... I caught you...

GOVERNOR: [*Escapes from him and runs around the stage.*] Golly! ...
            Help me out please... Help!

HOBOL: Catch the thief.

GOVERNOR: Back at you... Hey, Obol... Help me out...

HOBOL: [*Blocks the hostel's entrance.*] I won't let you escape.

The HUNTER *sticks his head out from among the suitcases. He hides
again among the suitcases after looking around and smiling.* OBOL
enters the stage. The GOVERNOR *has clung to the wall out of fear.*

GOVERNOR: [*As he sees* OBOL.] Obol... [*Runs and hides behind
            OBOL.*] He wanted to beat me... [*Pokes his head from
            behind OBOL.*] You deserve to be a thief yourself...

OBOL: What's going on here?

GOVERNOR: He called me a thief...

HOBOL: Mr Obol, call the police... He is the person who robbed
            me of all my stuff.

OBOL: Shut up! He's Mr Governor... [*To* GOVERNOR.] Don't
            bother yourself, sir...

HOBOL: Governor! ... Golly, I'm done.

GOVERNOR: [*Moves out from behind* OBOL.] It was you who called me a thief... eh? You are in for it.

HOBOL: I... I'm sorry... I...

OBOL: Shut your mouth... You did the hell...

HOBOL: Right... I did the hell... By the way, nuts to me...

GOVERNOR: [*Goes forward, stands quite next to* HOBOL, *and beckons to the pumpkin.*] What's this?

HOBOL: [*Picks the pumpkin up from the ground hurriedly. The* GOVERNOR *frightens and again runs toward* OBOL.] This... This is a pumpkin...

GOVERNOR: Pumpkin... Can't you pick it up in a civilized way?

OBOL: He's fastened it to himself in order not to get lost.

HOBOL: Yes... I was afraid if they'd rob me myself. They've robbed me of all my documents.

GOVERNOR: I got it now... So, you thought that I stole your documents. Say way to go. You're busted.

HOBOL: No... It was just a mistake... Anyway... how shall I say?

GOVERNOR: They looked like me... Am I right?

HOBOL: Yes... No... Let's forget about it... You know... just your clothes look like the thief... No, you aren't... I mistakenly took you for him.

GOVERNOR: Behave yourself... Pull yourself together.

HOBOL: Yes... Aye...

At this moment, OBOL *starts dialing a number. After a few seconds, phone ringing is heard from the* GOVERNOR's *office.*

GOVERNOR: It must be an important matter... People's demands should be handled... Aww, how funny it is!

The GOVERNOR *goes to the Governorate office in a hurry and closes the door behind him.*

OBOL: Aah! ... Why doesn't he answer? Hello? Yes, sir... Everything is ok... No, sir. I said that you won't accept anybody for nine months... Yes... Aye... [*Puts the receiver back.*]

HOBOL: It's too strange!

OBOL: Nothing is strange...

HOBOL: As if he was the one... How is it possible?

OBOL: [*To* HOBOL.] Did you notice that your goose was cooked?

HOBOL: Me! ... What's happened then?

OBOL: The Governor is too angry at you. He asked me to cancel the appointment I've made for you in nine months.

HOBOL: Golly! ... What shall I do now? I should surely meet the Governor.

OBOL: Do you mean despite the accusation you made against him?

HOBOL: It's not my fault... They resembled each other very much... Even their clothes were the same.

OBOL: Did you see all the thief's clothes?

HOBOL: Yes...

OBOL: Even his underclothes...

HOBOL: Underclothes? No, I couldn't... I mean he didn't show me.

OBOL: What about that of the Governor?

HOBOL: No...

OBOL: How strange! ... Well, you'd expect to see them... I mean the underclothes of such an honorable man...

HOBOL: No... Bugger me... I remembered now. The thief put on other clothes... They were just a bit similar. Maybe they'd worn no clothes...

OBOL: So many things look like each other in the town.

HOBOL: Right... I took them mistakenly...

The GOVERNOR *enters.*

GOVERNOR: He dialed the wrong number... He wanted someone else.

HOBOL:	How is it possible?! [*Approaches* OBOL.] Hey Obol, you talked with the Governor, didn't you?
OBOL:	None of your business... Is it possible that the Governor tells a lie?
HOBOL:	Not at all... I thought so... but you said that...
OBOL:	Yes, I did... I didn't tell a lie, did I? Get out of my way...
HOBOL:	How strange! ... [*Goes near the wall and murmurs to himself with a silly half-smile on his face.*] I'm out of my mind... [*Beats himself on the head and laughs loudly.*] Yeah... I'm crazy...

The HUNTER *laughs loudly.*

GOVERNOR:	Yes! ... Who is he?
OBOL:	They are preparing his room.
GOVERNOR:	He's a traveler then... How funny! ... [*Goes forward and tries to see the* HUNTER.] Hey... who are you?
HUNTER:	Me! ... Who are you then?
GOVERNOR:	[*Points at the signboard on the Governorate Office.*] Didn't you see? It says that...
HOBOL:	He is the Governor... You should make an appointment.
HUNTER:	It's closed... I saw it.
GOVERNOR:	[*Goes toward* OBOL.] Is it possible to open the office just for a few days?
OBOL:	No, sir... You are expected to be on vacation now.
GOVERNOR:	Well, who shall pay my salary?
OBOL:	I gave you what you wished, didn't I? You know that you couldn't easily go around and rest if I didn't provide you with hostel income. Where have you been today, for example?
GOVERNOR:	In the zoo... Do you know? The animals are growing day by day. I should send a Letter of Encouragement to the animal trainers in the zoo...
OBOL:	Sure... You'd better do it right today... because the zoo would be a good source of income for us.

HOBOL: Are there any orangutans in the zoo?

GOVERNOR: Orangutan? What does it look like?

OBOL: O'! ... Not only orangutan... but we've also managed to produce some new animal species by breeding.

HOBOL: Aah... How nice!

GOVERNOR: Yes... How funny they were! ... I saw one of them which was... I mean its head was like that of a wolf, its feet like that of a bear... You'd better see its belly! ... It was just like a cow belly... We talked with each other for a long time.

OBOL: This is just one out of so many models... You can find some new models if you keep on searching.

GOVERNOR: I also saw a winged cat... Poor canaries!

OBOL: Did they complain then?

GOVERNOR: Cats, no... but the canaries were so sad.

OBOL: You weren't supposed to talk with them... Had they made an appointment?

GOVERNOR: I felt pity for them.

OBOL: Maybe you're tired... because of working hard.

HUNTER: What if one day the door of all cages open?

The GOVERNOR *gets agitated and takes a look at* HOBOL *and the* HUNTER *in haste.* HOBOL *beckons to the* HUNTER.

HOBOL: He was the one... He says he was a hunter at first but now he's telling poems...

GOVERNOR: Hunter! ... But where is his head then?

HOBOL: Somewhere under there... Under the howdah, behind the suitcases...

GOVERNOR: He might get crushed under such a big howdah.

OBOL: He'd like to do so...

GOVERNOR: Poor guy! ... [*Touches the chair laying on the howdah.*] What a beautiful chair! ... May I sit on it?

OBOL: Not now... He should rest...

GOVERNOR: Since when have you carried this howdah on your shoulders?

HOBOL: He's been in this position since we saw him.

GOVERNOR: So, we'd better leave him on his own... have mercy on him, and not mess with him.

HOBOL: He doesn't hurt anybody either... He can only keep on thinking under the suitcases... He knows some stories as well.

GOVERNOR: Story! ... What kind of story?

HOBOL: The story of a champion who's got stuck in a loop.

GOVERNOR: How was that? ... I like stories...

OBOL: It isn't worth hearing.

HOBOL: Yes... don't take it seriously... It was somehow nonsense.

GOVERNOR: It's not something new... As if I've read or heard it again and again... [*Goes toward the Governorate office, pauses for a while, then turns his back.*] Didn't he say what happened at the end of the story?

HOBOL: The end of it?! No... I don't remember... Maybe it had no end.

GOVERNOR: There is... Every story has an end...

OBOL: But its end depends on us...

HUNTER: [*Moves.*] No... Everybody makes it end in a certain way.

OBOL: Who allowed you to talk?

HOBOL: [*Excitedly.*] Oh! ... He's the same hunter.

GOVERNOR: [*To the HUNTER.*] What are you doing down there?

HUNTER: I think... I think about the end of the story.

GOVERNOR: Well... how's it going to end?

HUNTER: For whom?

GOVERNOR: It doesn't differ, does it? Where there is a Governorate office that...

HUNTER: It's closed... You're going too far...

GOVERNOR: Not at all, sir… It's too serious… If I get my hands on you…

The WAITRESS *enters.*

WAITRESS: No… I don't know why there should be so many pebbles among the rice grains!

GOVERNOR: Oh, you again…

WAITRESS: No… I have no idea where all these pebbles have come from…

GOVERNOR: [*Approaches the* WAITRESS.] Haven't you removed the pebbles from the rice grains yet?

WAITRESS: No… I can no longer see clearly.

GOVERNOR: Yeah…, you look older for your age… You don't have sharp eyes anymore.

OBOL *gets busy dialing a number. Telephone ringing is heard from the* GOVERNOR's *office.*

GOVERNOR: Golly! … Don't they know the Governorate office is closed for the time being?

The GOVERNOR *hurries into the Governorate office.*

HOBOL: How dog-eat-dog it is. I'm going crazy again…

OBOL: Hello… Hi, sir… Yes, wait a moment… You have an appointment… at 6 a.m. … Yes… Due to the high volume of work… Aye. [*Puts the receiver back.*]

WAITRESS: I don't know if there is a secret why I can't finish with removing the pebbles from the rice grains?

HUNTER: Don't bother yourself… Any secret takes time to come out… and it's not the right time for it.

WAITRESS: As it's clear from your voice, you've not eaten food.

HUNTER: Yeah… I'm about to starve.

OBOL: Ok… I should tidy up here… [*To the* WAITRESS.] Get up, go and sit on your own seat… [*Begins shouting as he sees the* WAITRESS *is still sitting.*] I told you to get up and go…

WAITRESS: [*Gets up and begins walking.*] It's dark in the kitchen... I can see nothing clearly...

HOBOL *drags his heels for a while, then puts the pumpkin on the ground and walks a few steps. The pumpkin is dragging on the ground. He picks it up again and sits on the couch.*

OBOL: Hey, Hobol...

HOBOL: Huh? What's up?

OBOL: [*Beckons HOBOL over.*] Come on... Come here...

HOBOL *goes a few steps forward and then stops.* OBOL *beckons* HOBOL *over again and he goes closer.*

OBOL: Rent...

HOBOL: Aye... Here you are... [*Takes a large amount of money out of his pocket.*] I have much more if you want...

OBOL: How much?

HOBOL: Plenty...

OBOL: Do you know what the hell would happen to you if I throw you out of here? You would be robbed of your pumpkin.

HOBOL: No... please... I have nowhere else to go...

OBOL: But I don't need money...

HOBOL: Don't you? But I've got nothing else.

OBOL: Here is the waiting hall... You can't hang out here a long time... You have to work for me if you want me not to throw you out...

HOBOL: Aye... I'll do whatever you say.

OBOL: We need much more investment to develop the zoo... I mean, to make much more money and develop the hostel...

HOBOL: Aye... Accidently, I like animals very much... especially, orangutans...

OBOL: Well done, good boy... Now you've got a name... but a name without any title is of no use... I should find a title for you.

HOBOL: Title! … Good idea… How would it be then?

OBOL: You wouldn't have to carry this pumpkin with yourself wherever you go.

HOBOL: Do you mean that I wouldn't get lost anymore?

OBOL: No… I myself prepare an ID for you… [*Turns to the Governorate office.*] It's a long time the Governorate office has been left closed… Don't you feel hungry?

HOBOL: I do…

OBOL: Ok… Let's go to the kitchen… [*Points at the* HUNTER.] I should get rid of him as I return… I feel bothered in his presence.

They leave the stage together. The HUNTER *moves. He gets out his head smoothly and carefully from behind the suitcases. When sure that nobody is around, puts the howdah on the ground, puts his hand on the couch, pillar and wall, and goes to the door of the Governor's office… He knocks on the door.*

HUNTER: Hey… open the door.

GOVERNOR: I can't… My plan has been scheduled by my office assistant…

HUNTER: Come out… I've also come out from beneath the howdah.

GOVERNOR: I can't do it right now… I have an appointment.

HUNTER: Poor guy… You'll be in for it if you don't come out…

GOVERNOR: Back at you… Now then, I'll tell my assistant to give you the last room… No, get out of here. There's no vacant room here.

HUNTER: I've figured out the end of the story… I'll tell you if you wish.

GOVERNOR: Wow! … Sounds great. I'd really like to know it but my assistant should schedule an appointment for you…

The WAITRESS *enters. As they see each other, both stop for a few seconds and look at each other. The* HUNTER *goes toward the* WAITRESS *a few steps and smiles. Hearing approaching footsteps, the* HUNTER *begins stumbling toward the howdah and gets under it. The* WAITRESS *also takes shelter in a corner.* OBOL *enters and goes toward the* HUNTER.

OBOL: Give it a rest, can't you? Ok! … [*Goes behind the counter and takes the stick.*] Why don't you talk anymore? Say something… [*Hits the* HUNTER *on his leg several times with the stick.*] You might not see but you can hear instead… Answer me. [*Keeps on hitting the* HUNTER *madly again and again.*] Answer me… I said to answer me…

WAITRESS: Leeches…

OBOL: [*Notices the presence of the* WAITRESS.] Yes… are you here?

WAITRESS: What the hell do you want from him?

OBOL: I told you to go to the kitchen, didn't I? [*Goes toward the* WAITRESS *threateningly.*]

WAITRESS: I said it's dark there… I can see clearly… [*Steps back in a semi-circular shape till she reaches the* HUNTER.]

OBOL: Seems you're getting above yourself…

WAITRESS: It's dark…

OBOL: Shut up!… [*Hits on the tray with the stick and pours the rice on the ground. The* WAITRESS *hides behind the* HUNTER.]

HUNTER: You're a total shit! …

OBOL: Sounds great… You've begun talking at long last… Huh? Here it is… [*Beats the* HUNTER *with the stick.*]

Hearing the clamor outside, the GOVERNOR *comes out and goes immediately toward* OBOL *to stop him.*

GOVERNOR: What are you doing? Leave him alone… [*Grabs the stick.*]

OBOL: [*Stands still just for a moment.*] What's happened?

GOVERNOR: Have mercy on him… He's tied up.

OBOL: [*Pulls the stick out of the* GOVERNOR's *hand.*] Don't get into it... I'm the manager here.

GOVERNOR: It's not ok to behave towards the clients this way, Mr Obol...

OBOL: No need to help him... You're in dire need of help yourself... Get out of my way.

The GOVERNOR *looks at the* WAITRESS *desperately, then sits next to her.*

WAITRESS: You know nothing about here... He doesn't allow me to remove pebbles from the rice... You know nothing...

The WAITRESS *gets up and leaves the stage slowly.*

GOVERNOR: You're too bad... I must have known you from the very beginning.

OBOL: You're right, Mr Governor... but now it's too late...

GOVERNOR: Late?

OBOL: Would you like to know why? Wait. I'll tell you now... [*Goes behind the counter and opens a big notebook on it.*] Come on... Look here... You should take care of these documents.

GOVERNOR: Which documents? I should review them.

OBOL: No need to do so... According to these documents, your debts are piling up so much that you can't pay even half of them although you have a lifetime of hard work.

GOVERNOR: What should I pay? Where have these documents come from?

OBOL: Well, it seems you know nothing about them... Running the Governorate office costs a lot; cost of renting the building, transportation... pocket money....

GOVERNOR: Oh! ... You've put all on my account, haven't you?

OBOL: Sure thing! ... Shall I pay the costs out of my own pocket while the Governorate office is closed?

GOVERNOR: I don't accept responsibility for them...

OBOL: According to these documents, you owe me… and I have to obey the rules. [*Takes out the special file of the Appointment Letters.*] Look… You've signed them all, haven't you?

GOVERNOR: Oh! … I didn't think that…

OBOL: Yeah… According to this Appointment Letter, you made me responsible for maintaining and running here. You also said that I should obey the rules.

GOVERNOR: Yes… I still abide by them… Rules are the first priority… [*Browses through the file.*] What is this then?

OBOL: How come that you don't remember? This is the first Appointment Letter you gave me.

GOVERNOR: Yeah… I remember… You came and asked me to employ you as a waiter… Right… Then all the rooms in this building were related to the Governorate… By the way, what happened that you suggested to consider one of the rooms for the poor helpless travelers?

OBOL: To help the town economy and attract tourists.

GOVERNOR: Right… You well remember it… Then we fired all the clerks, emptied the rooms one by one, and rented them instead.

HUNTER: You, poor guy! … Your sin is your very first mistake that gave him the first Appointment Letter…

GOVERNOR: Were you talking with me?

HUNTER: Yeah… Now you are a Governor who has been enslaved by his own employee… [*Laughs.*] How ridiculous!

OBOL: Why don't you come out?

HUNTER: Come out? [*Laughs.*] Come down here if you'd like to see me…

GOVERNOR: [*To* OBOL *with a childish happiness.*] I had your number… Now I go to open my office and nullify all the Appointment Letters… [*Laughs loudly.*] I feel a great relief… I'll show you who you're dealing with… How funny!

OBOL: [*Calmly.*] You can't enter that room anymore... You should pay off all your outstanding rents first...

GOVERNOR: You're all wet... Here is still considered the Governorate building.

OBOL: I've bought here.

GOVERNOR: Do you mean the Governorate building?

OBOL: Here is its deed... Your debts are now due. According to the law, I could order you to be imprisoned if you refuse to pay them.

GOVERNOR: [*To himself in astonishment.*] Has he bought the Governorate building?

OBOL: Anyway it would happen one day.

HUNTER: But it might not happen.

OBOL: But it did happen... It's over... Now I'm the owner of here... [*To the* GOVERNOR.] You have to resign...

GOVERNOR: Do I have to?

HUNTER: Yeah... you have to... You have to atone for it... And what a pity that many people are ignorant about the situation in this town.

GOVERNOR: No... I'm still the Governor...

OBOL: You've already fallen from grace... Hobol would kill you if I arrived late... Who knows? Maybe he was right...

GOVERNOR: You mean that I'm a thief. How is it possible?

OBOL: People don't tell lies...

GOVERNOR: Lie, no... but...

OBOL: But what? Seems you want to accuse them of stupidity and malevolence too... Right?

GOVERNOR: No... but I can say that they'd made a mistake.

HUNTER: Hey... I want to talk...

OBOL: Say what you wish... Nobody can hear you... but come out and let me know who you are...

HUNTER: No... I fear... because not everybody is himself... All have worn the same clothes, robbed the name of the noble people, and carried anything by taking advantage of their credit. Anyway, they can be seen but not known... They've lost themselves...

OBOL: That's it? [*To the* GOVERNOR.] Well, nothing lasts forever... [*Puts a paper in front of the* GOVERNOR.] Here you are... Sign it.

GOVERNOR: [*Gets the paper and reads it.*] "I would like with great pleasure to resign friendly due to fatigue, and go for a long rest in order to get fully recovered. So, I really wish a great success for my dearest, Mr Obol." It's both illegible and grammatically incorrect... By the way, don't think that I didn't get it... The word "Success" doesn't start with letter C and the word "Dear" doesn't start with letter T.

OBOL: None of your business... Sign and finish it.

GOVERNOR: No... Never.

OBOL: There's no way out... You've got no place and no one anymore... According to the rules, you can no longer be Governor... Your presence here is somehow considered a kind of renouncing of the rules... This town is no longer as before... Your time is over. [*Picks up a rope and approaches the* GOVERNOR.]

GOVERNOR: What are these ropes for?

OBOL: Don't you know?

GOVERNOR: No... I wanted to ask a few times but you talked about different things and I forgot about it.

OBOL: The rooms at the end of hallway...

OBOL *leaves the stage while sniggering. The* HUNTER *drags his heels for a while and then goes out slowly.*

HUNTER: So tight is the loop of the fate and champion,
Got stuck in the hardship noose of time.

GOVERNOR: Oh! ... Did you get out?

HUNTER: [*Gets refreshed by moving his head, neck, and hands.*] I
know... I know they would pollute the earth and help
the extinction of human generation when they come
into power.

GOVERNOR: As if there are so many things you're aware of.

HUNTER: Yeah... That's why I wouldn't like to show myself and
face Obol... I've heard a lot of words, and thought
about all of them... Yeah... nothing could stop me
thinking although they obstructed my view... I can no
longer tolerate carrying this load... I've held this
howdah on my shoulders for a lifetime and carried its
owner and her suitcases. The wounds on my
shoulders... will be always with me.

GOVERNOR: Leave them alone and go out if you think that you can
no longer pull it off.

HUNTER: Where? Among all those animals you've produced?

GOVERNOR: The choice is yours... but don't stay here... I began to
doubt Obol's behavior.

HUNTER: Really? How did you know? [*While laughing, goes a few
steps forward. But he twists his ankle and falls down.*]
Ouch!

GOVERNOR: Aah! ... [*Goes forward.*] What's happened? [*Grabs the
HUNTER's hand. The HUNTER gets up.*] Why did it
happen?

HUNTER: I should get used to it and believe the feet are mine.

GOVERNOR: [*Laughs.*] How funny! ... When you fell down, you
looked like the baby wild boar which was born today. It
also fell down as it began moving.

HUNTER: Really? But I'm a hunter.

GOVERNOR: O'! ... So, that stupid guy was right, wasn't he?

HUNTER: Yeah... Those animals you've bred will be
uncontrollable very soon... Do you know what would
happen if the door of all cages open one day? [*Walks a*

few steps and falls down.] Ouch! ... I should walk without those loads...

GOVERNOR: Give me your hand... [*Holds out his hand.*]

HUNTER: [*Holds out his hand to grab the* GOVERNOR's *hand, but changes his mind and pulls back his hand.*] No... I should learn to get up on my own... [*Gets up with difficulty.*]

The WAITRESS *enters with a sweeper in her hand.*

WAITRESS: The floor must be cleaned.

HUNTER: [*Goes toward the* WAITRESS.] Can I help you?

GOVERNOR: Uh... You'd better leave here.

HUNTER: Right... but first of all I must know what there are in these suitcases that I've tolerated the weight of for a lifetime.

GOVERNOR: Have they all been always closed?

HUNTER: Yeah... They belong to that fat woman. What do you think is inside them?

GOVERNOR: How shall I know? They've been on your shoulders...

HUNTER: It's time... to know what there is inside them.

WAITRESS: Nobody would ever like to know a pile of pebbles is among the rice grains.

HUNTER: [*Finds a screwdriver and goes toward the suitcases. Falls down once, but gets up.*] I must know what the secret of the heavy weight of these suitcases is... [*Inserts the screwdriver into the lock of one suitcase and pushes it.*]

GOVERNOR: How good it would be if there's something valuable inside them... Can I help you?

HUNTER: It's my own load... I should open it myself... [*The suitcase opens. It's empty and seems very light.*] It's empty!

GOVERNOR: Gee! ... There's nothing in it...

HUNTER: [*Opens another suitcase.*] This is empty too! ... Well, that fat woman! ... It was them that have enslaved me a lifetime! ... Empty and heavy suitcases! ... The suitcases which have no destination!

GOVERNOR: [*Picks up one of the suitcases.*] It's too light...

WAITRESS: [*While collecting rice grains.*] No... they look the same in appearance... but at the time of cooking, it gets clear that... [*Pours a handful of collected rice grains into the tray.*]

HUNTER: [*Kicks over the suitcases angrily.*] They are all lies... It goes for all the goods in this town... Empty and heavy suitcases...

WAITRESS: If anybody can see, of course! ... All the rice grains would be crushed under their feet in darkness.

GOVERNOR: How careless you are! ... You've been under these suitcases a lifetime and didn't notice they were empty?

HUNTER: Many people don't know they are always carrying the weight of empty suitcases on their shoulders... I feel I can breathe better now... I know that outside with all its hardship is better than staying here...

GOVERNOR: How funny! ... I'll come with you.

HUNTER: Where will you go with me? I'm going to the animals... Your load is too heavy... It's too hard for you to get rid of it.

WAITRESS: [*While sweeping the floor.*] With all these pebbles and dirt mingled with rice grains, it takes a long time to remove them.

GOVERNOR: First of all, I must take care of the documents... Obol took whatever I had...

The HUNTER *goes and stands over the* WAITRESS. *They look at each other for a while and exchange smiles. Then step toward the hostel's entrance.*

WAITRESS: [*Sweeps.*] The ground wouldn't be easily cleaned.

The HUNTER *twists his ankle and falls down as he reaches the hostel's entrance. He gets up with difficulty and leaves the hostel. The* WAITRESS *is still busy sweeping the ground. The* HUNTER's *footsteps are sporadically heard from behind the stage, mixed with the rustle of sweeping by the* WAITRESS.

The stage darkens suddenly.

Ends.

www.ingramcontent.com/pod-product-compliance
Lightning Source LLC
LaVergne TN
LVHW041310080426
835510LV00009B/938